10 FOR $10 SHEET MUSIC

Classical Piano Arrangements

CONTENTS

Cover Image: Sheet music © istockphoto.com/trigga

Copyright © MMX by Alfred Music Publishing Co., Inc.
All Rights Reserved   Printed in USA

Alfred

ISBN-10: 0-7390-7332-X
ISBN-13: 978-0-7390-7332-2

1812 OVERTURE

Peter Ilyich Tchaikovsky (1840–14893)
Op. 49
Arranged by Carol Matz

Moderately fast

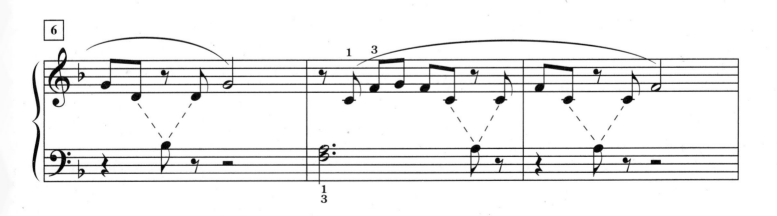

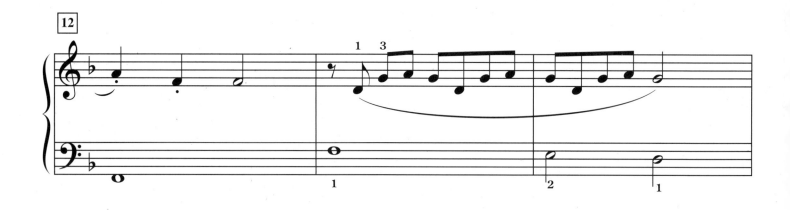

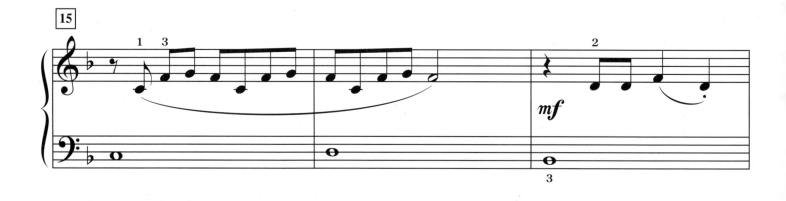

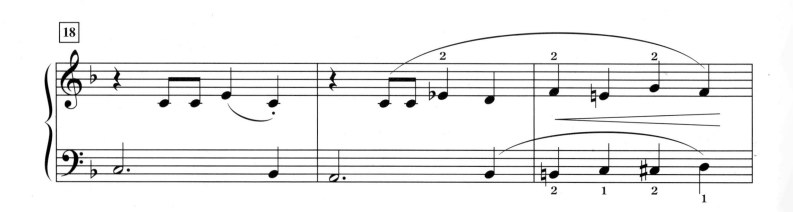

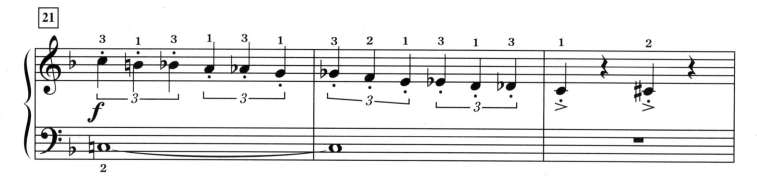

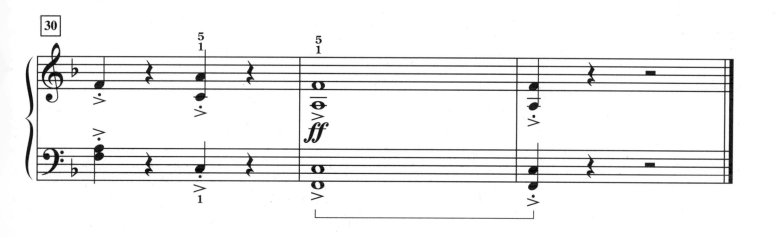

CELLO SUITE NO. 1 IN G MAJOR

(Prelude)

Johann Sebastian Bach (1685–1750)
BWV 1007
Arranged by Bruce Nelson

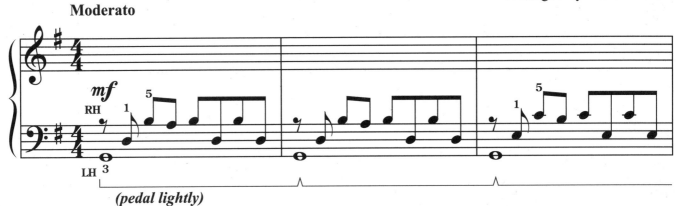

Moderato

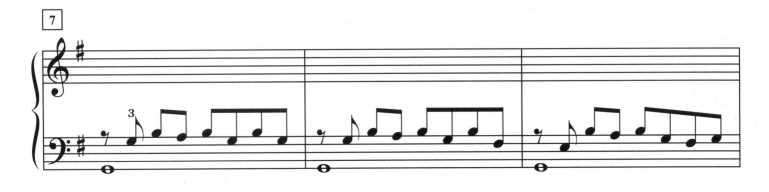

simile

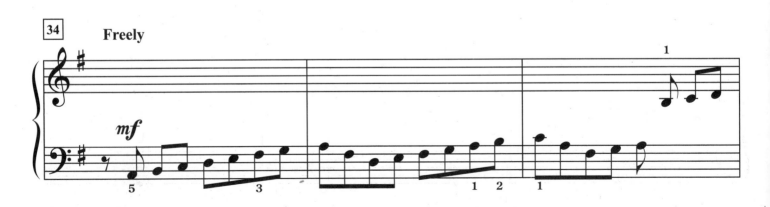

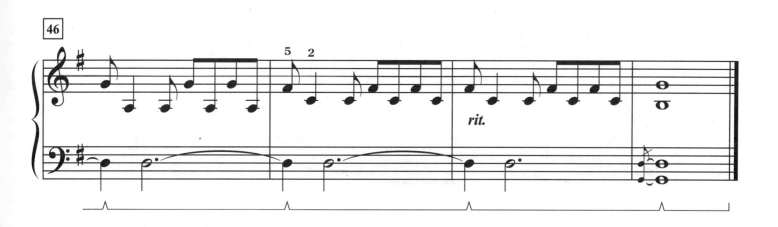

CLAIR DE LUNE

(from *Suite Bergamasque*)

Claude Debussy
(1862–1918)
Arranged by E. L. Lancaster

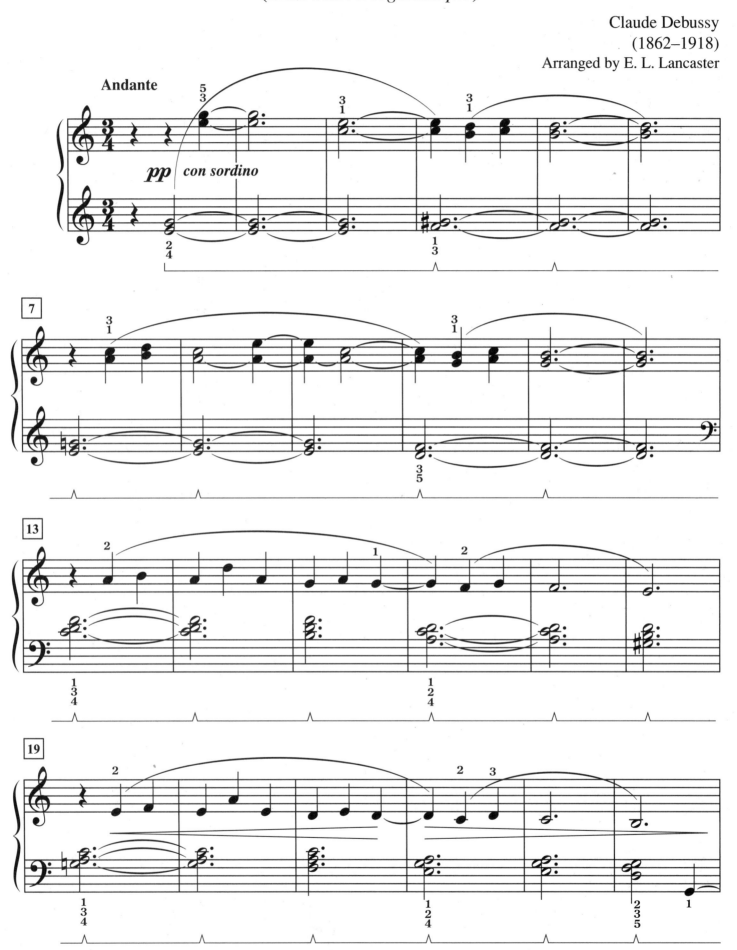

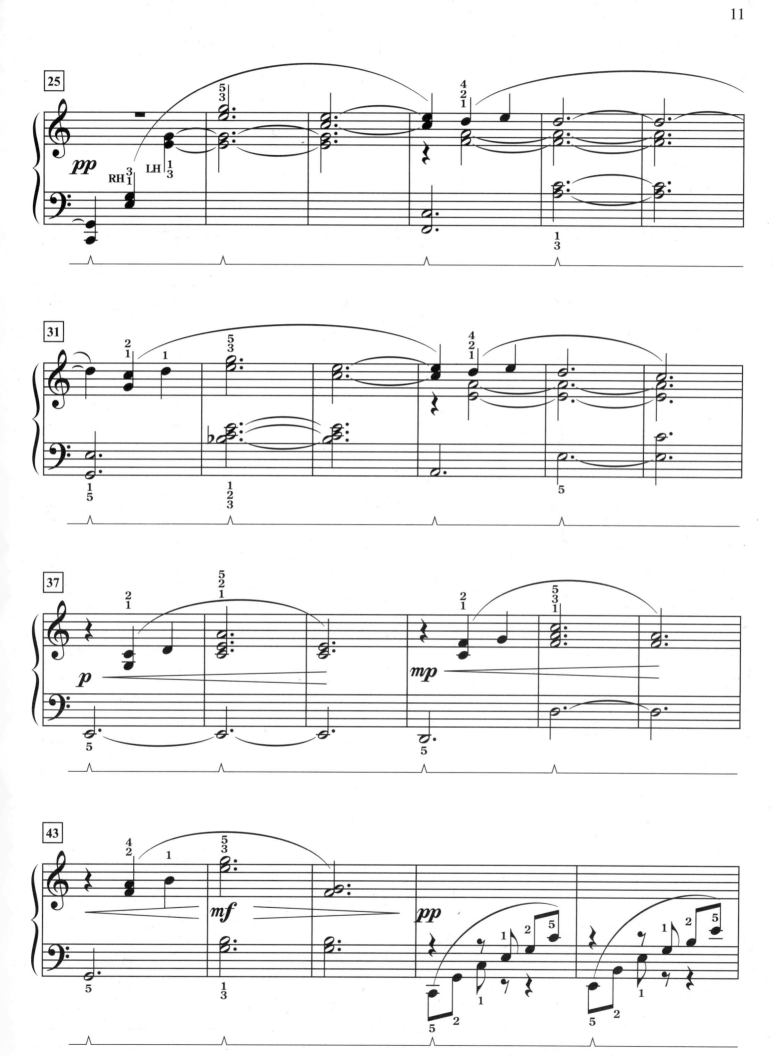

EINE KLEINE NACHTMUSIK

(First Movement)

Wolfgang Amadeus Mozart (1756–1791)
K. 525
Arranged by Mary K. Sallee

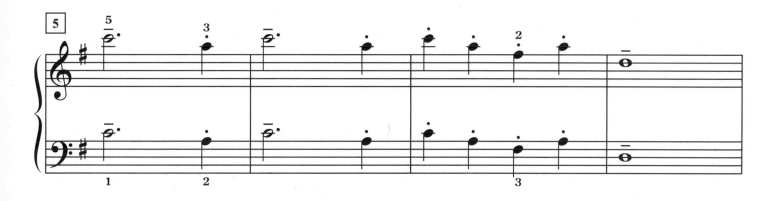

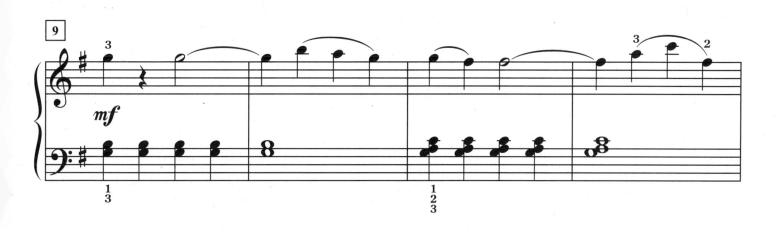

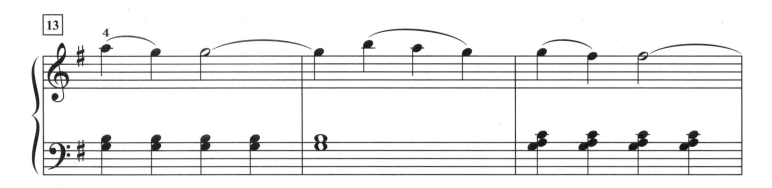

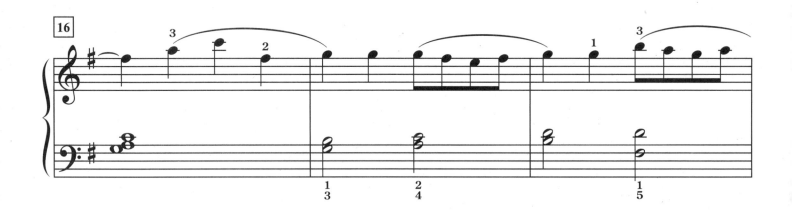

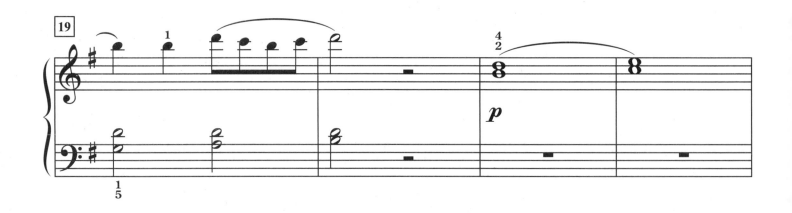

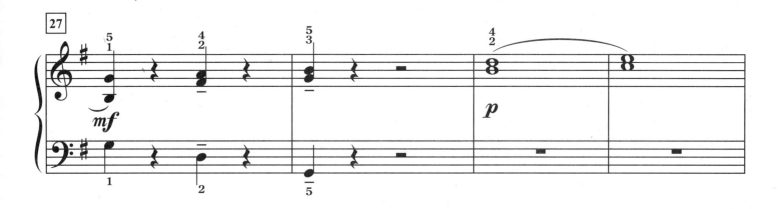

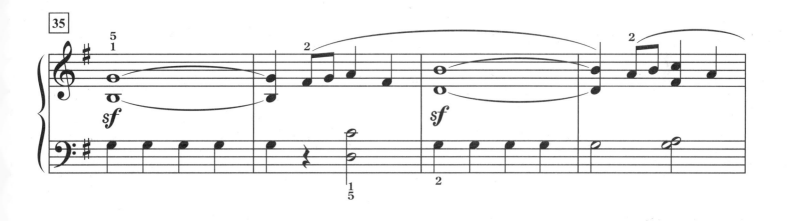

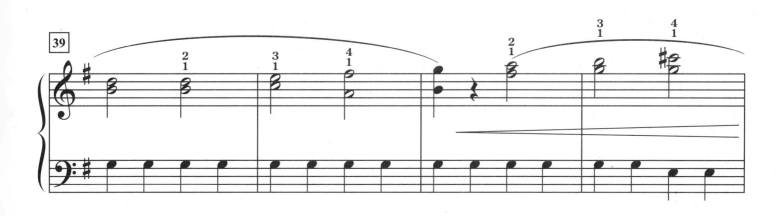

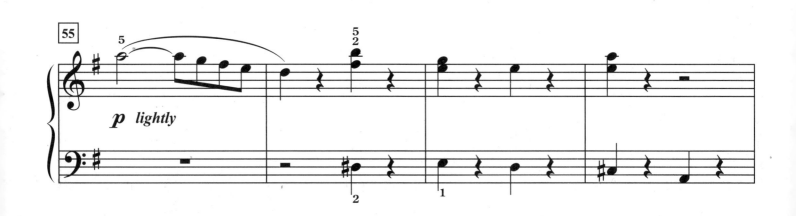

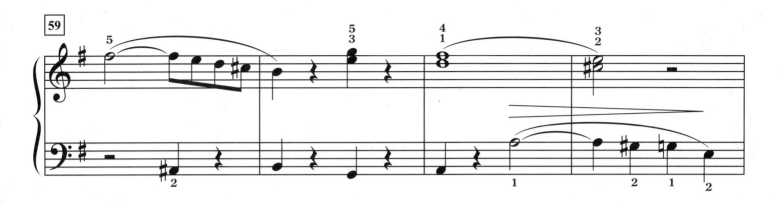

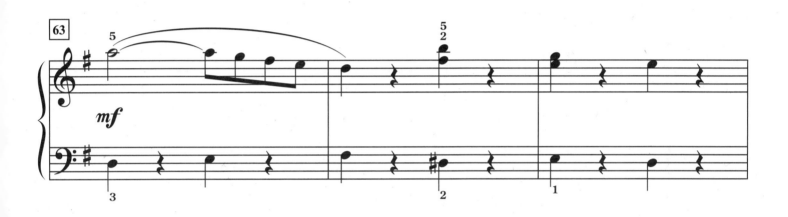

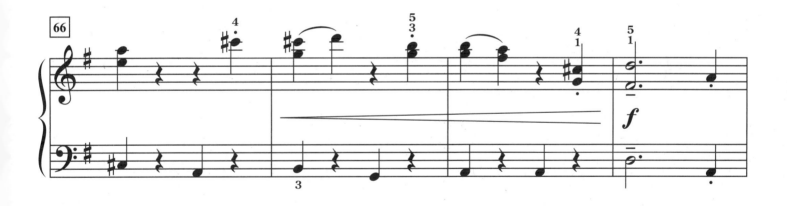

MOONLIGHT SONATA

(Piano Sonata No. 14, First Movement)

Ludwig van Beethoven (1770–1827)
Op. 27, No. 2
Arranged by Mary K. Sallee

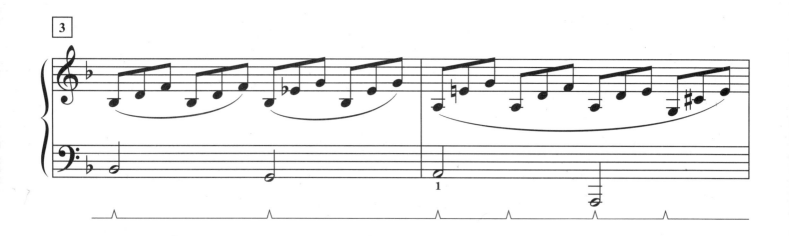

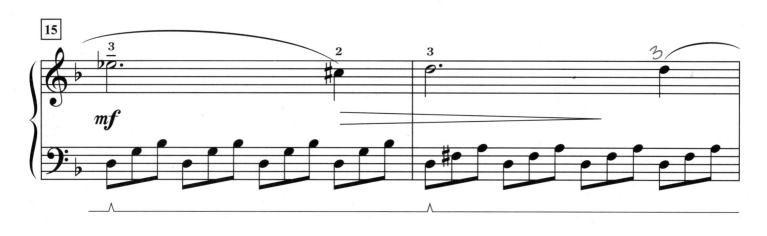

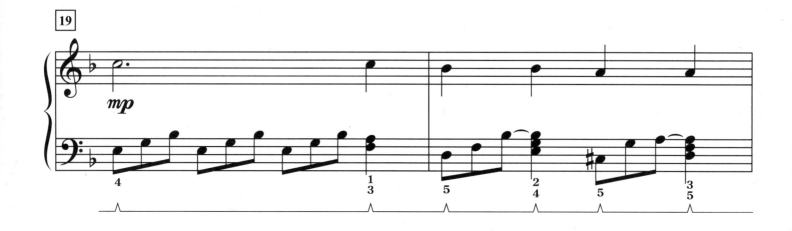

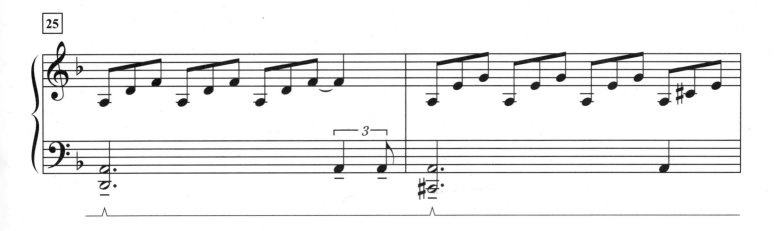

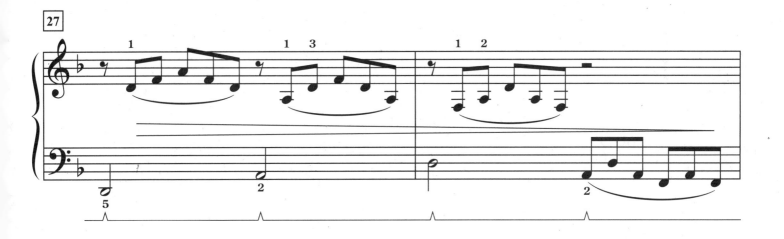

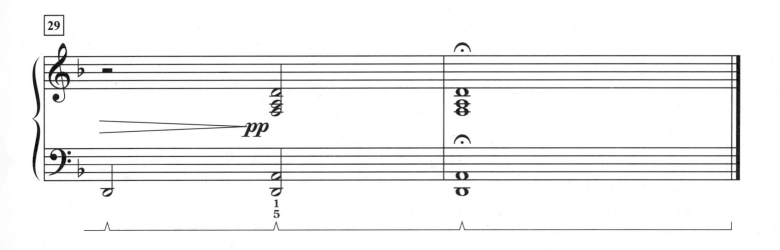

QUEEN OF THE NIGHT ARIA

(from *The Magic Flute*)

Wolfgang Amadeus Mozart (1756–1791)
K. 620
Arranged by Tom Gerou

Allegro assai

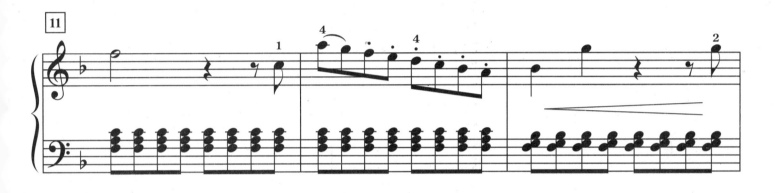

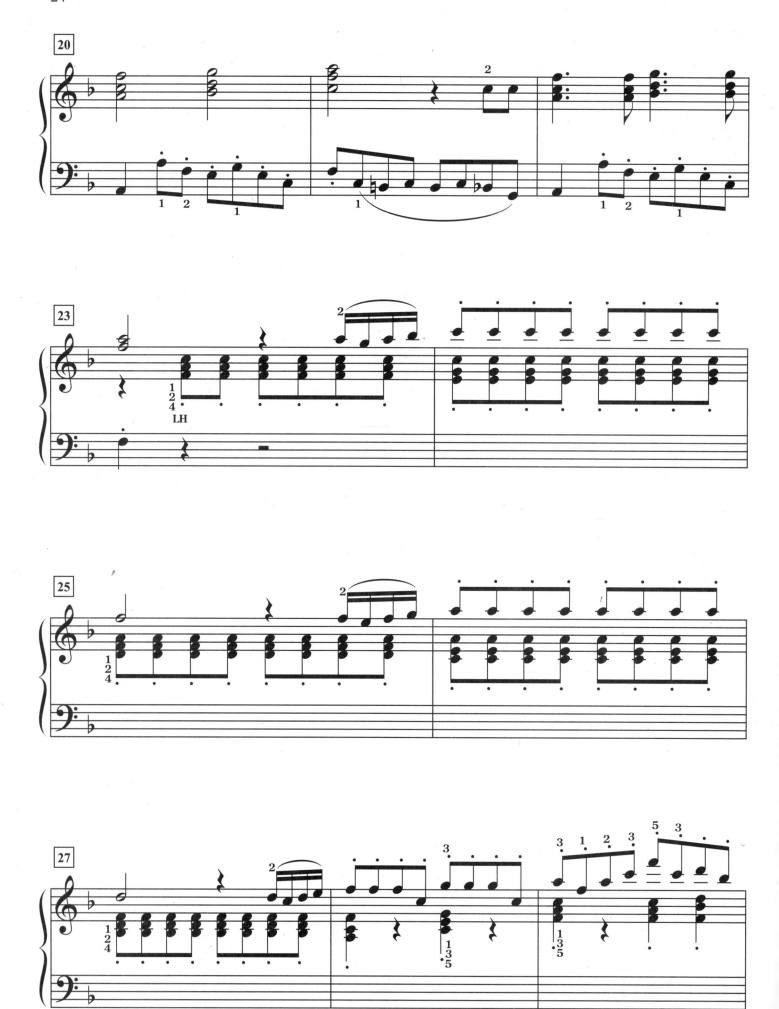

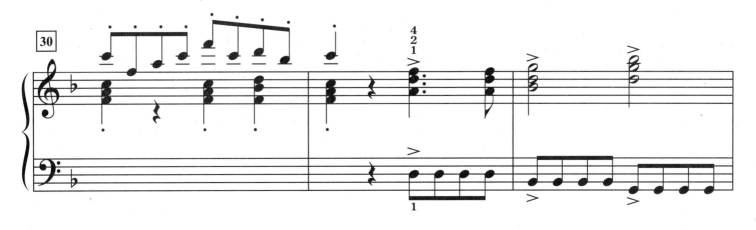

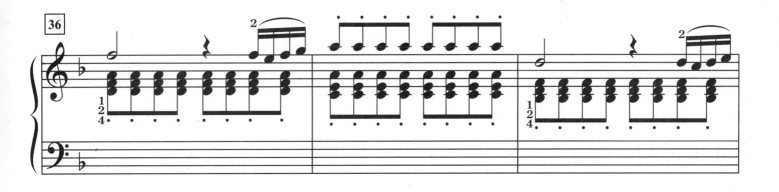

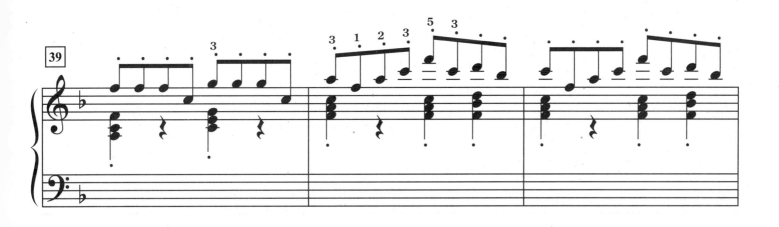

REVOLUTIONARY ETUDE

Frédéric Chopin (1810–1849)
Op. 10, No. 12
Arranged by Jerry Ray

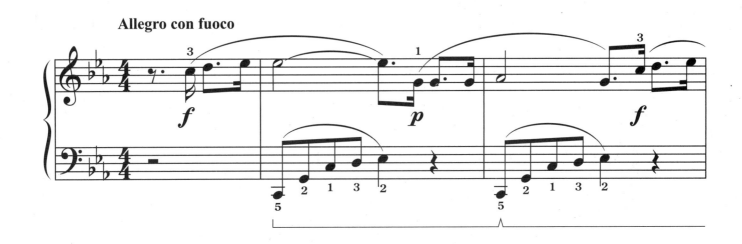

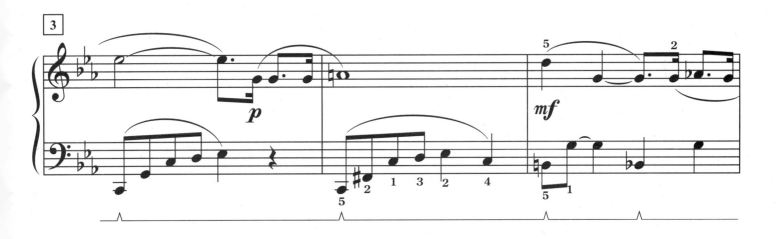

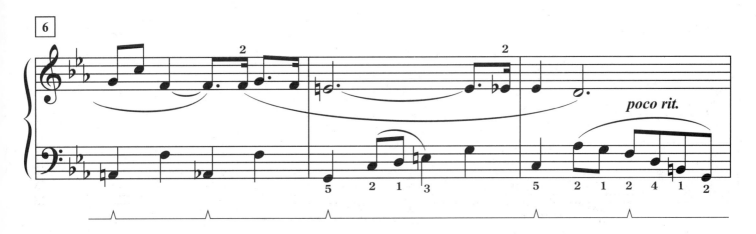

RONDO ALLA TURCA

(Piano Sonata No. 11, Third Movement)

Wolfgang Amadeus Mozart (1756–1791)
K. 331
Arranged by Mary K. Sallee

With haste, in two

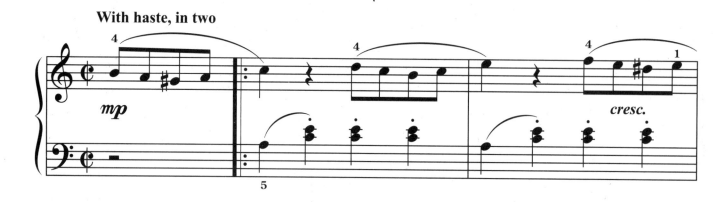

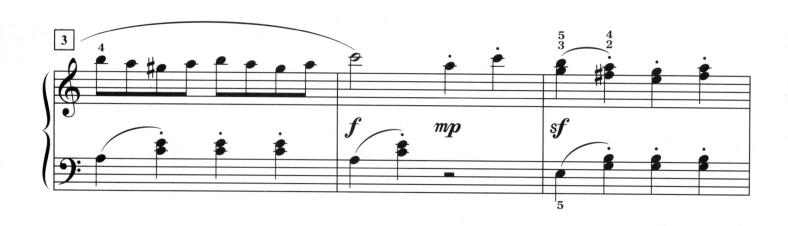

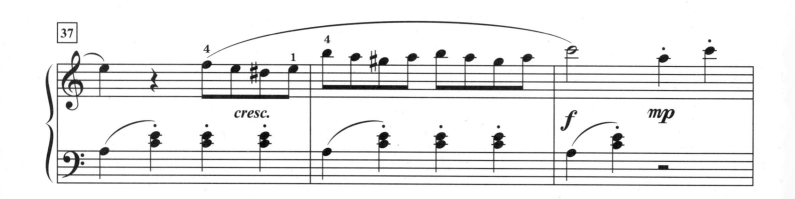

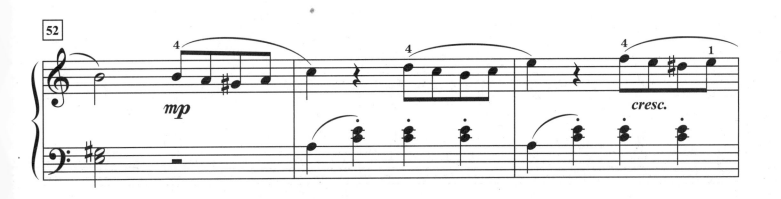

THE SORCERER'S APPRENTICE

Paul Dukas
(1865–1935)
Arranged by Robert Schultz

Animato

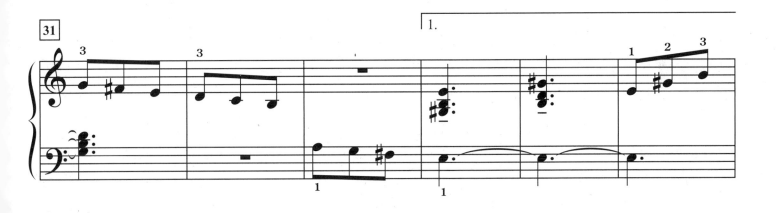

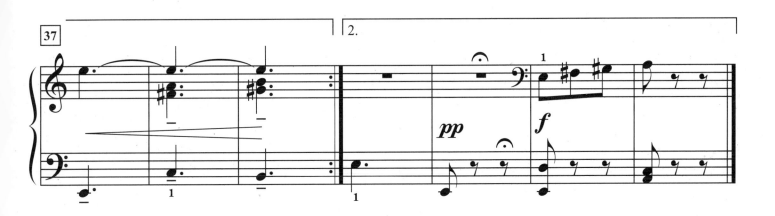

SPRING

(from *The Four Seasons*)

Antonio Vivaldi (1678–1741)
Op. 8, No. 1, RV 269
Arranged by Bruce Nelson

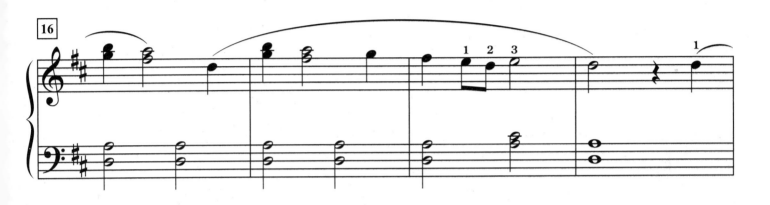

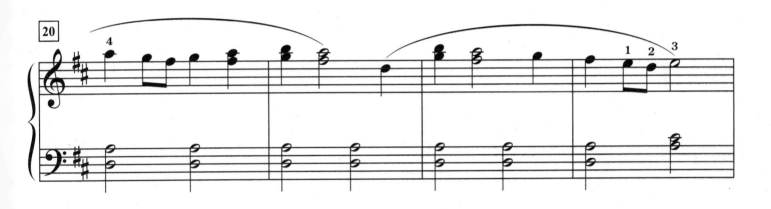

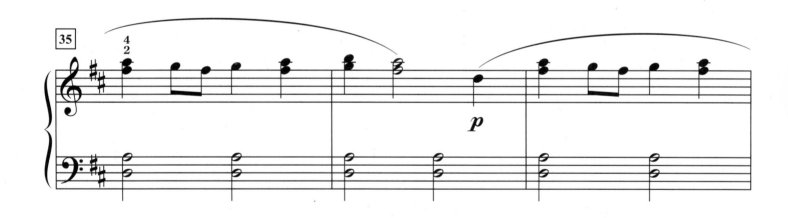